This book belongs to

....

To my daughter, Keira,
who always wanted her own dog,
which inevitably made me write this book

And inspired by my mom
and her love for the written word

–M.S.

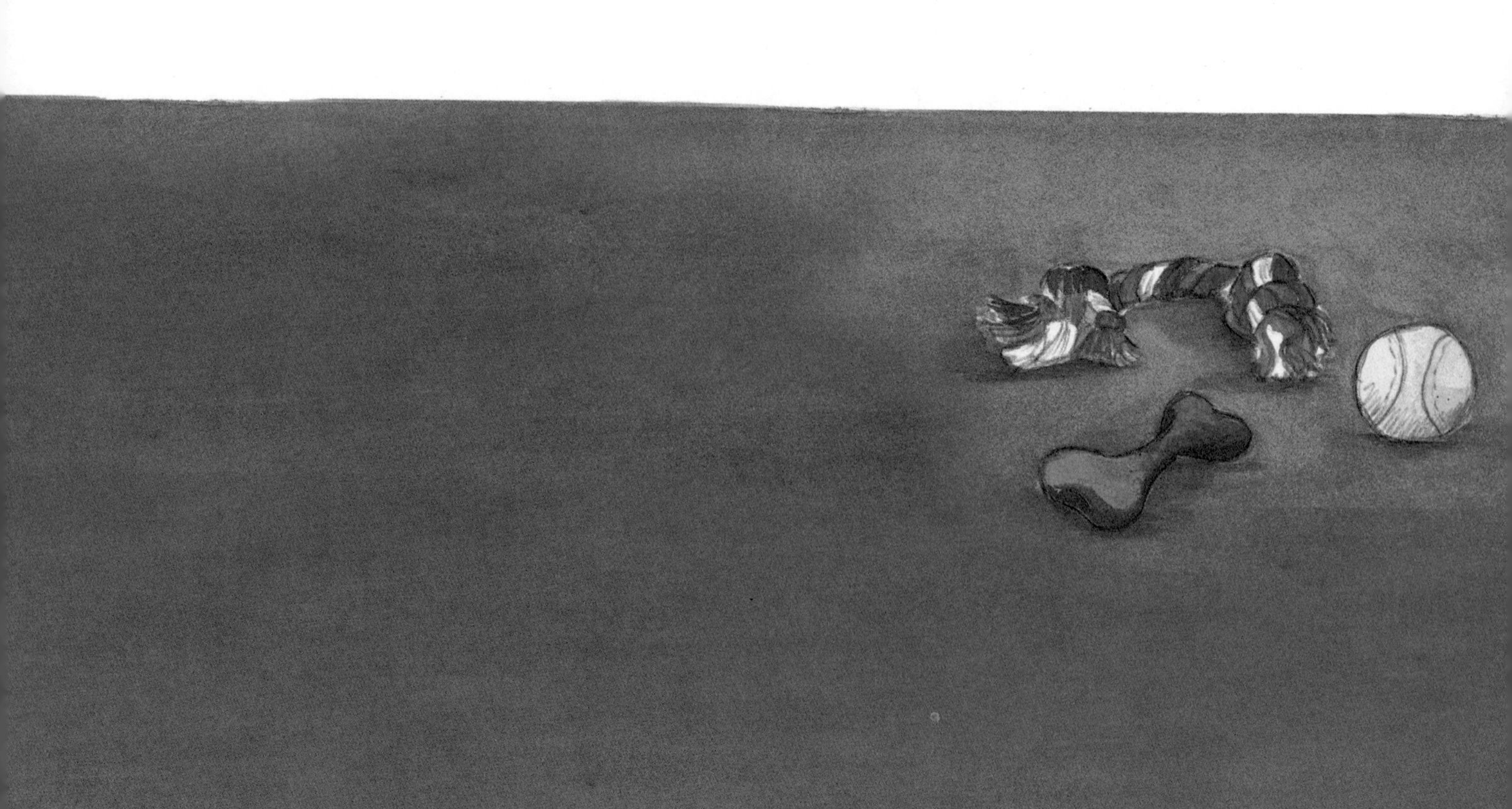

What to Know Before You Get Your Dog

MARGRIT STROHMAIER

Illustrated by Claudia Gadotti

ADOPT
WITH
ADOPT
TODAY

Before you get a dog,
ask yourself in every way:
Do I know what doggies need?
Do I know how doggies play?

A dog is not a toy.
This should be very clear.
And just like you and me,
dogs see and feel and hear.

DOG FOOD
Pet Shop

You may already know,
dogs love to play and eat.
They please their owner, then…
they hope to get a treat!

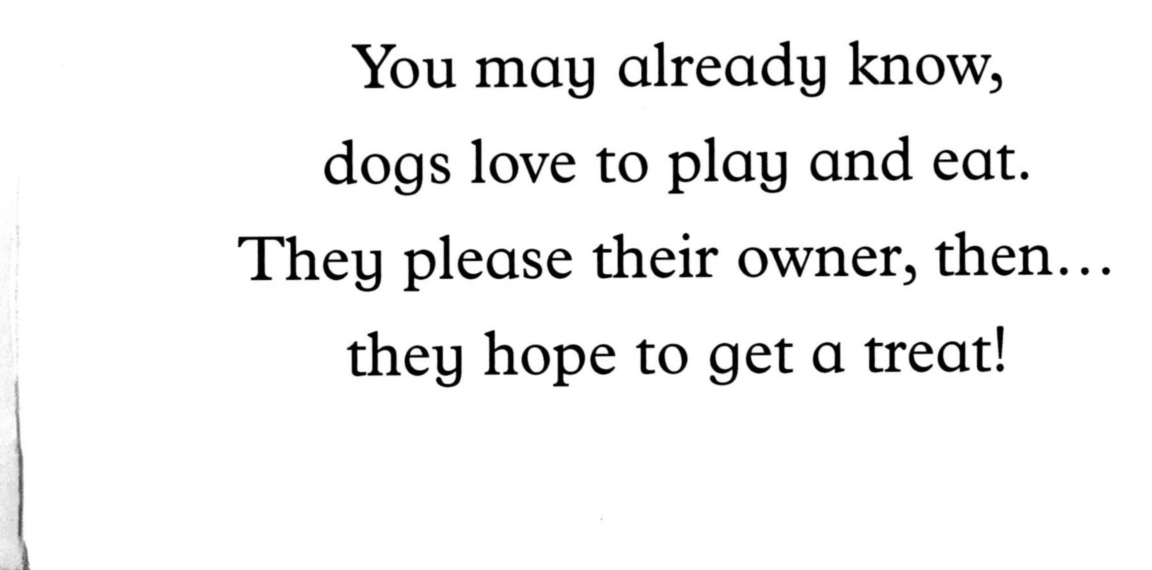

You'll have to teach a dog
commands like come and stay,
and how to sit and wait
until it's time to play.

A special game will be
to teach a dog a trick…
to run outside and chase
a ball or wooden stick.

You'll need to walk a dog
or take him for a run…
to play with other dogs,
to romp and have some fun.

But when a dog gets bored,
he looks for things to do.
And if you're not around,
he may destroy your shoe.

That's why you'll need to put
your clothes and things away,
but leave the doggie toys
so he can play all day.

You'll need to take a dog
for visits to the vet...
for check-ups, shots and care,
a must for every pet!

A dog who's home alone
is sad, but he will learn...
He won't be lonely long.
His family will return.

You'll need to give a dog
a place to rest and sleep...

a blanket or a bed,
and lots of toys to keep.

DOG
FOOD

You'll also need to learn
to pick up doggie poo, ew!
To feed and keep him clean
is something you must do.

The most important thing,
no matter what their breed,
is giving lots of cuddles
and all the love they need.

All this will be some work,
but will be worth your while.
A dog that feels so loved
will always make you smile.

Before you get a dog,
ask yourself in every way:
Am I ready for this job?
Can I do this every day?

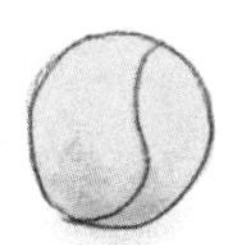

That's why you need to know
for sure—and please don't guess:
Are you ready for YOUR dog?

And is your answer _____?

Margrit Strohmaier has always been an animal lover. She was inspired to write her first picture book, *What to Know Before You Get Your Dog*, by her daughter's relentless campaign to have her own dog. Margrit's passion for creativity and art, along with her desire to raise her daughter's awareness about the responsibility of dog ownership, resulted in the creation of this award-winning book.

Margrit has a Bachelor of Fine Arts degree and is the recipient of the Ana Blanc Verna Award for Creative Thinking. Originally from Austria, Margrit now resides in Connecticut with her family and their fluffy dog, Scruffy.

Visit her @ www.margritstrohmaier.com

Claudia Gadotti comes from Trento, Italy. She has always been a book lover and always wanted to be an illustrator. She has a degree in Fine Arts with a major in Illustration from the Academy of Art University in California and has been an illustrator for 15 years. She lived in London, then California, and now she resides in Auckland, New Zealand, with her husband and two dogs.

Copyright © 2021 by Margrit Strohmaier

All rights reserved. No part of this book may be reproduced or used in any manner without the prior written permission of the copyright owner, except for the use of brief quotations in a book review.

First Edition 2021

Illustrations by Claudia Gadotti
Book Design by Praise Saflor

Publisher's Cataloging-in-Publication data

Names: Strohmaier, Margrit, author. | Gadotti, Claudia, illustrator.
Title: What to know before you get your dog / Margrit Strohmaier ; illustrated by Claudia Gadotti.
Series: What to Know Before...
Description: Westport, CT: Lion Face Press, 2021. | Summary: An illustrated, rhyming picture book that teaches kids about the joys and commitment of dog ownership.
Identifiers: LCCN: 2021907415 | ISBN: 978-1-7369995-2-3 (hardcover) | 978-1-7369995-0-9 (paperback) | 978-1-7369995-1-6 (ebook)
Subjects: LCSH Dogs--Juvenile literature. | CYAC Dogs. | BISAC PETS / Dogs / General
Classification: LCC SF426.5 .S77 2021 | DDC 636.7--dc23

Thank you for reading my book!

Visit www.margritstrohmaier.com to download your own copy of the Dog Care Contract and Chore Chart.

DOG CARE CONTRACT

I, ________________, promise to take care of my dog, ____________, and give him/her love, care and attention throughout their entire life. I promise to always treat him/her kindly and gently, and to do everything I can to provide a safe, clean, comfortable, healthy and happy home.

If I am younger than 6 years old, I promise to:

- help my parents prepare food and water for my dog.
- help my parents walk my dog.
- clean up my toys, but leave the dog toys out for my dog to play with.
- help my parents play with my dog.
- give my dog lots of love every day.

If I am over 6 years old, I also promise to:

- give my dog priority over my iphone, iPad, TV, Xbox or other non-priority things.
- make sure my dog has fresh water at all times.
- help to make a healthy meal for my dog each day.
- spend time playing with my dog each day.
- help train my dog to behave well.
- help walk my dog and clean up after him/her.
- help give my dog a bath and brush him/her on a regular basis.
- give my dog lots of love.

Child's Signature: ________ Parent's Signature: ________

Date: ________ Date: ________

MY DOG'S CARE CHART

Name:

SUN	MON	TUE	WED	THU	FRI	SAT

If you enjoy this book, it would mean the world to me if you write a review on Amazon. Your kind feedback is much appreciated and so very important.

Thank you so much for your time.

Margrit

Made in the USA
Middletown, DE
20 August 2022